ALL ABOUT DINOSAURS

PARASAUROLOPHUS

BookLife

by

Mike Clark

©2018
Book Life
King's Lynn
Norfolk PE30 4LS

ISBN: 978-1-78637-181-2

Written by:
Mike Clark

Edited by:
Charlie Ogden

Designed by:
Matt Rumbelow

A catalogue record for this book
is available from the British Library.

PHOTO CREDITS

Abbreviations: l-left, r-right, b-bottom, t-top, c-centre, m-middle.
Front Cover – Catmando. P2-3: bg – Aqnus Febriyant; front – Warpaint. P4-5: bg – goory. P4: front – Catmando. P5: front – Warpaint. P6-7: iurii. P8-9: bg – kaesunza. P8: l – MarcelClemens; r – guysal. P9 – Lisa Andres/wikipedia. P11: front Ralf Juergen Kraft; back – Catmando. P12-13: w bg – ZoranKrstic; front – Andreas Meyer. P14-15: Catmando. P15: D. Gordon E. Robertson. P16-17: i am way. P16: Catmando. 17: topimages. P18-19: l – Warpaint; m: Herschel Hoffmeyer; r: Warpaint. P20-21: l – Ralf Juergen Kraft; r – Luis Molinero. 24: Catmando. Images are courtesy of Shutterstock.com. With thanks to Getty Images, Thinkstock Photo and iStockphoto.

CONTENTS

Words that appear like this can be found in the glossary on page 23.

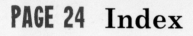

WHAT WERE DINOSAURS?

Dinosaurs were reptiles that lived on Earth for over 160 million years before they went extinct.

There were many different types of dinosaur. They lived both on land and in water – and some could even fly!

WHEN WERE DINOSAURS ALIVE?

Dinosaurs first lived around 230 million years ago during a period of time called the **Mesozoic** period. The last dinosaurs went extinct around 65 million years before humans were alive.

Millions of years ago, all the land on Earth was together in one piece. But during the time of the dinosaurs, it slowly broke up into the different continents that we know today.

WHEN ALL THE LAND ON EARTH WAS TOGETHER IN ONE PIECE, IT WAS CALLED PANGEA.

PANGEA

HOW DO WE KNOW ...?

We know so much about dinosaurs thanks to the scientists, called palaeontologists (pay-lee-on-tol-uh-gists), who study them. They dig up **fossils** of dinosaurs to find out more about them.

EGG

FOSSIL

Scientists put together the bones they find to try to make full dinosaur skeletons. From these skeletons, scientists can often work out the size and weight of a dinosaur. We can also find out information about what it ate from fossilised food and poo.

PARASAUROLOPHUS SKELETON

SCIENTISTS HAVE EVEN FOUND FOSSILISED EGGS AND FOOTPRINTS BELONGING TO DINOSAURS.

THE PARASAUROLOPHUS

The Parasaurolophus had one of the strangest skulls of any dinosaur. It had a large, horn-shaped bone sticking out of the back of its head. This is called a crest.

NAME	Parasaurolophus (par-ah-sawr-ol-uh-fus)
LENGTH	9–11 metres
HEIGHT	3.5 metres
WEIGHT	2500 kilograms
FOOD	HERBIVORE
WHEN IT LIVED	65–76 million years ago
HOW IT MOVED	Walked on two legs
WEAPONS	Long, thick tail

The Parasaurolophus lived over 65 million years ago. It lived during the same time as the Albertosaurus (al-ber-tuh-sawr-us), which would have tried to eat the Parasaurolophus.

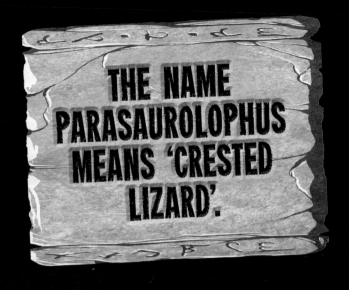

THE NAME PARASAUROLOPHUS MEANS 'CRESTED LIZARD'.

ALBERTOSAURUS

CREST

WHAT DID THE PARASAUROLOPHUS LOOK LIKE?

The Parasaurolophus had a thick tail that it used to defend itself. It would have swung its tail to fight off **predators**, such as the Albertosaurus.

12

The Parasaurolophus also had a large crest on the back of its head. Palaeontologists believe the crest might have helped the dinosaur to keep cool in hot weather.

WHERE DID THE PARASAUROLOPHUS LIVE?

Parasaurolophus fossils have been found in the United States of America and in Canada. Palaeontologists believe that these places were warm swamps during the time of the Parasaurolophus.

Canada

U.S.A

Some palaeontologists believe that the Parasaurolophuses lived in **herds**. Some palaeontologists also think that groups of these dinosaurs moved huge distances during the year in order to stay in warm weather. This is known as migrating.

Parasaurolophus Skull

WHAT DID THE PARASAUROLOPHUS EAT?

The Parasaurolophus was a herbivore, meaning that it only ate plants. It probably would have looked for food in swamps.

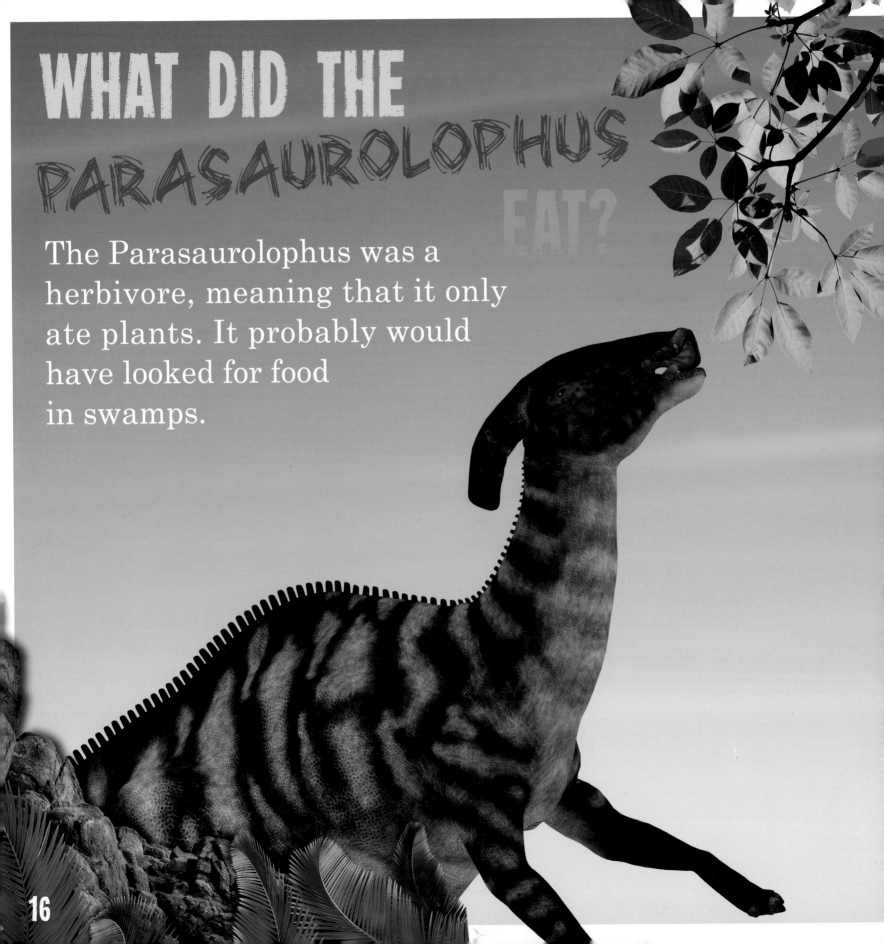

The Parasaurolophus had large, flat teeth. It would have used these teeth to grind grass and leaves.

Teeth used for eating plants.

DID THE PARASAUROLOPHUS HAVE THE STRANGEST SKULL?

The Parasaurolophus had a very strange skull. However, it was not the only dinosaur with a strangely shaped head.

The Triceratops (try-sair-uh-tops) had two large horns on the top of its head and a large frill around its neck. It also had one of the largest skulls of any dinosaur.

The Pachycephalosaurus (pak-ee-sef-uh-lo-sawr-us) had a large, bowl-shaped skull that was covered in small spikes.

FACTS ABOUT THE
PARASAUROLOPHUS

LARGE CREST

FLAT, GRINDING TEETH

ONE-AND-A-
HALF-METRE
LONG SKULL

350 CM METRES TALL.

THICK TAIL, USED TO SCARE AWAY PREDATORS

170 CM TALL

LONG BACK LEGS, USED FOR REACHING LEAVES

FIND THE
PARASAUROLOPHUS'
TWIN

GLOSSARY

continents very large areas of land that are made up of many countries, like Africa and Europe

extinct a word used to describe a species of animal that is no longer alive

fossils the remains of very old plants and animals that lived a long time ago

herbivore an animal that only eats plants

herds large groups of animals that live together

Mesozoic a period of time when dinosaurs lived

predators animals that hunt other animals for food

reptiles cold-blooded animals with scales

swamps lands flooded with a shallow layer of water

INDEX